HAVE FUN READING THIS BOOK!

IT OFFERS SOME REAL **SURVIVAL TIPS**. BUT THE SETTINGS **ARE NOT REAL**. **THINK** ABOUT HOW YOU CAN USE THESE **HACKS** IN REAL LIFE. USE **COMMON SENSE**. **BE SAFE** AND **ASK** AN **ADULT** FOR **PERMISSION** AND **HELP** WHEN NEEDED.

45th Parallel Press

Published in the United States of America by Cherry Lake Publishing
Ann Arbor, Michigan
www.cherrylakepublishing.com

Reading Adviser: Marla Conn, MS, Ed., Literacy specialist, Read-Ability, Inc.
Book Designer: Felicia Macheske

Photo Credits: © Artur. B/Shutterstock.com, cover; © Sebastian Kaulitzki/Shutterstock.com, 5; © AstroStar/Shutterstock.com, 6; © Ebtikar/Shutterstock.com, 9; © Aaron Amat/Shutterstock.com, 11; © Tyler Boyes/Shutterstock.com, 13; © B-D-S Piotr Marcinski/Shutterstock.com, 14; © BeataGFX/Shutterstock.com, 15; © M Kunz/Shutterstock.com, 17; © Slava_Kovtun/Shutterstock.com, 17; © donatas1205/Shutterstock.com, 19; © Ilja Generalov/Shutterstock.com, 21; © mirtmirt/Shutterstock.com, 22; © Dino Osmic/Shutterstock.com, 25; © robert_s/Shutterstock.com, 27; © New Africa/Shutterstock.com, 29

Other Images Throughout: © SrsPvl Witch/Shutterstock.com; © Igor Vitkovskiy/Shutterstock.com; © FabrikaSimf/Shutterstock.com; © bulbspark/Shutterstock.com; © donatas1205/Shutterstock.com; © NinaM/Shutterstock.com; © Picsfive/Shutterstock.com; © prapann/Shutterstock.com; © S_Kuzmin/Shutterstock.com © autsawin uttisin/Shutterstock.com; © xpixel/Shutterstock.com; © OoddySmile/Shutterstock.com; © ilikestudio/Shutterstock.com; © Kues/Shutterstock.com; © Artur. B/Shutterstock.com, © ankomando/Shutterstock.com

45th Parallel Press is an imprint of Cherry Lake Publishing.

Library of Congress Cataloging-in-Publication Data

Names: Loh-Hagan, Virginia, author.
Title: Alien invasion hacks / by Virginia Loh-Hagan.
Description: Ann Arbor, MI : Cherry Lake Publishing, [2019] | Series: Could you survive? | Includes bibliographical references and index.
Identifiers: LCCN 2019006163| ISBN 9781534147812 (hardcover) | ISBN 9781534150676 (pbk.) | ISBN 9781534149243 (pdf) | ISBN 9781534152106 (hosted ebook)
Subjects: LCSH: Survival—Juvenile literature. | Extraterrestrial beings—Juvenile literature. | Human-alien encounters—Juvenile literature.
Classification: LCC GF86 .L6424 2019 | DDC 613.6/9—dc23
LC record available at https://lccn.loc.gov/2019006163

Cherry Lake Publishing would like to acknowledge the work of The Partnership for 21st Century Skills. Please visit *www.p21.org* for more information.

Printed in the United States of America
Corporate Graphics

Dr. Virginia Loh-Hagan is an author, university professor, former classroom teacher, and curriculum designer. She's written 45th Parallel Press books about aliens. For example, she wrote about Roswell. She lives in San Diego with her very tall husband and very naughty dogs.

COULD YOU SURVIVE AN ALIEN INVASION?

THIS BOOK COULD SAVE YOUR LIFE!

Aliens are also called **extraterrestrials**. This means they're from outside Earth. Aliens are from outer space. They come from other planets. They come from other worlds. They may even come from other **solar systems**. Solar systems are made up of the sun and all the objects that **orbit** it. Orbit means circle around.

There's so much we don't know about space. Scientists say our sun is 1 of 200 billion stars. What if we're not alone in this universe? What if aliens are looking for us too?

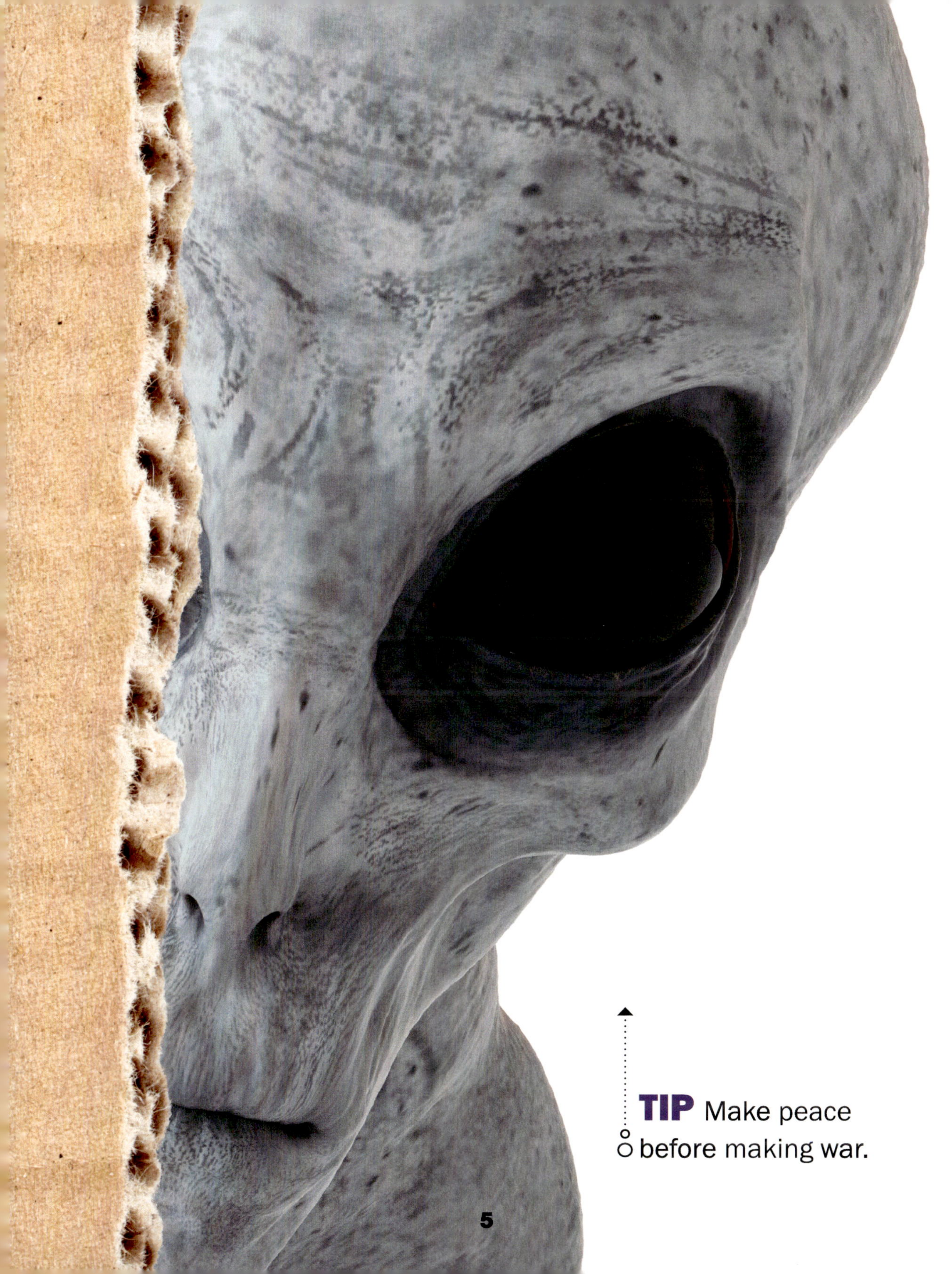

TIP Make peace before making war.

One day, aliens could invade Earth. They may be looking for a new home. They may want to take Earth away from us. Or they may just want to destroy Earth.

We don't know what aliens want. We don't speak their language. We don't know anything about them. It will be hard to win a war against aliens.

Some people think aliens want to turn humans into slaves. Others think aliens want to kill humans. Either way, we're in trouble. Their technology is better than ours.

TIP Get a telescope. Scan the sky.

Aliens have landed. They're attacking. Our human armies are no match. Our weapons are light-years behind their weapons. But you might be one of the lucky survivors. You have to be smart. Study aliens. Learn as much as you can about them. Find their weaknesses. Figure out what they want. Focus on hiding and staying alive.

Most importantly, know how to survive. Keep this in mind:

- You can only live 3 minutes without air.
- You can only live 3 days without water.
- You can only live 3 weeks without food.

This book offers you survival **hacks**, or tricks. Always be prepared. Good luck to you.

TIP Stay calm. Don't panic. If you panic, you can't think.

SCIENCE CONNECTION

Mars is called the Red Planet. It looks like a red star. The red comes from the rust in Martian rocks. It has a lot of dust storms. It's a dry and dusty planet. It's the fourth planet from the sun. This means it's cold. The weather is similar to Antarctica. The nights are really cold. It's too cold for life to grow. The air is 100 times thinner than on Earth. There isn't enough oxygen. Humans couldn't breathe on Mars. In general, it'd be hard for life to thrive on Mars. Mars's surface has a lot of bad rays. There's not much water. Scientists are looking for life on Mars. They send out study missions. So far, there haven't been any signs of life. But there have been some possibilities. A study found some salty water near the surface. Another study found signs of a large lake. The lake was hidden beneath many layers.

CHAPTER 1

TAKE A DEEP BREATH!

Oh no! Aliens may **infect** the air. Infect means to make others sick. Aliens may change the air. They may do this to make things more comfortable for themselves. You'll need to go outside to get things. Make an air mask. It's better to be safe than sorry.

TIP Stay inside as long as you can.

HACK

1. Get a 2-liter soda bottle.
2. Cut out the side. Make it fit your face. Turn the bottle upside down. The top of the bottle should be by your chin. Keep the cap on it.
3. Stuff the cut area with wet cloth. This is where your nose and mouth will go
4. Attach it to your face. Seal it with **duct tape**. Duct tape is special tape. It's strong. It's flexible. It keeps water and air out.

TIP Cover up. Skin can absorb poison.

explained by STEM

The key to this hack is the wet cloth.

The wet cloth acts as a **filter**. Filters let things pass through. The holes in the cloth need to be small enough to let water pass but not let germs in. Layer the cloth enough to keep bad things out. But don't layer too much so that you can't breathe.

Cloth is made of **fibers**. Fibers are tiny threads. Water swells the fibers. It makes the holes smaller. It fills in empty spaces. This keeps more bad things out. Bad things get trapped in the fibers. Water also makes cloth able to absorb things without clogging.

CHAPTER 2

GLOW IN THE DARK!

You'll need light to get around at night. Also, some stories say aliens don't like water. Make water that glows. And, if you have to, throw it at the aliens. Then run!

HACK

1. Get a clear jar with a lid. Fill it with **tonic water**. Tonic water is a type of soda.
2. Get highlighter pens. Yellow works the best.
3. Uncap the pens. Pull the ink tube out.
4. Put the ink tube in the cup. Let the ink bleed into the water. The ink should change the water color.
5. Mix the water and ink. Put the lid on the jar.
6. Shine a black light at the water. Do this in the dark. The water will glow.

TIP Don't take selfies with aliens. Run and hide!

explained by STEM

The key to this hack is the black light.

A black light shines **UV** light rays. UV means ultraviolet. These are special rays. Humans can't see them. Highlighter dyes have **phosphors**. Tonic water has **quinine**. Both phosphors and quinine are substances. They glow under a black light. The black light excites the phosphors and quinine. The phosphors and quinine take in the light energy. They turn UV rays into light we can see. They return back to their normal state.

Don't look directly at the black light. Don't shine it on your skin. The black light can hurt your eyes and skin.

TIP Use black light to find alien slime.

REAL-LIFE CONNECTION

Jody Pendarvis believes in aliens. He lives in Bowman, South Carolina. He built a welcome center. He built it in his backyard. He built it in 1994. He did this to welcome aliens. He wanted aliens to feel at home. He wanted to give them a place to rest after their long space journey. The welcome center is shaped like a 42-foot-wide (13-meter) flying saucer. It's built of wood, metal, and plastic. It's built on a powered ramp. It's mounted on 4 large poles. It goes up and down. It has a bed. It has a TV. It has air-conditioning. It has a toilet. It has a shower. It has small doors all over for aliens to enter. Pendarvis built a smaller spaceship. He added it to the welcome center. He built it just in case aliens wanted to take him with them.

CHAPTER 3

BAKE IN THE SUN!

You have to eat. You need strength to fight aliens. Make a **solar** oven. Solar means sun. Use power from the sun.

TIP Stock up on water and food.

HACK

1. Get a pizza box.
2. Draw a square on the top. Leave 1 inch (2.5 centimeters) on the edges. Cut out 3 sides. Make a flap.
3. Glue foil on the inside flap.
4. Glue foil at the bottom. Glue black paper on the bottom foil.
5. Tape plastic wrap over the open top. It should be under the foil flap.
6. Open the lid. Tape another piece of plastic wrap. Make an **airtight** window. Airtight means no air can get through.
7. Line the inside with newspaper.
8. Put under direct sun. Adjust the foil flap. Find the best angle for the sun. Use a stick to hold up the flap.

explained by

STEM

The key to this hack is the design.

The design makes and keeps heat. It transfers the sun's heat to the oven. The foil reflects sunlight into the oven. The black paper at the bottom absorbs sunlight. It takes in heat. It doesn't reflect it. This makes the oven warm. The plastic wrap window keeps the oven airtight. This means warm air doesn't leave through **convection**. Convection is the transfer of heat by the movement of air. The newspapers **insulate**. Insulate means to keep heat in.

This solar oven can reach about 200 degrees Fahrenheit (93 degrees Celsius). It can reheat food. It can take all day to make food.

TIP Don't use a solar oven to cook raw meat.

CHAPTER 4

JUICE IT UP!

Use your phone to call for help. Use it to get information. Keep it charged. Make your own **battery** with lemons! A battery is a source of power. But be careful. Aliens may be controlling our technology.

TIP Turn on all your technology. Jam up the aliens' signal.

HACK

1. Roll a lemon on a table. Loosen up the juice.
2. Get zinc nails or steel paper clips. Push into one end of the lemon.
3. Get a copper wire or coin. Push into the other end of the lemon.
4. Make sure copper and zinc don't touch.
5. Use another copper wire to connect the zinc and copper.
6. Do this for 30 lemons. Connect them all together with copper wire.
7. Cut open your phone's charging cord. Connect exposed cables to a copper wire.

TIP Keep track of alien movements and actions.

explained by

STEM

The key to this hack is the lemon juice.

Lemon juice is an **electrolyte**. Electrolytes carry electric charges. Batteries stop working when there aren't enough electrolytes. The lemon battery is made of 2 different metals. The metals act as **electrodes**. Electrodes take electric charges to or from a power source. The metals react. This makes power. More lemon batteries make more power. The copper wires serve as bridges.

Other fruits could be used. Examples are oranges, grapefruits, and potatoes. Be careful. This lemon battery could damage your phone. But it's better than nothing.

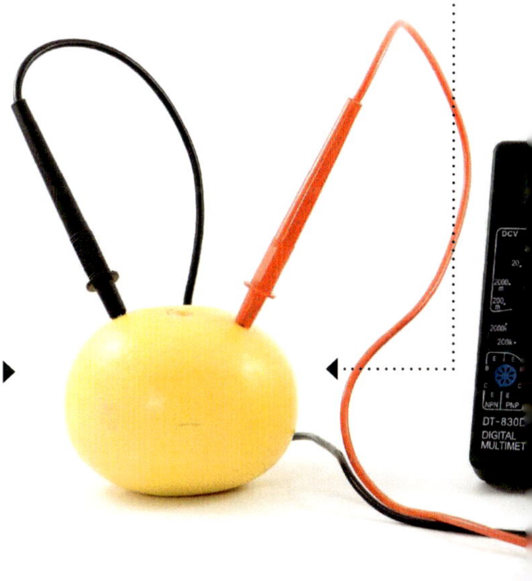

SPOTLIGHT BIOGRAPHY

Does life exist beyond Earth? Dr. Mary A. Voytek is interested in this question. She works for NASA. NASA is the National Aeronautics and Space Administration. It's in charge of the U.S. space program. Voytek became the leader of the astrobiology program in 2008. Astrobiology is the study of life on Earth and in space. Her job is to look for life on exoplanets. Exoplanets are planets whose orbits start outside our solar system. Voytek said, "Everyone is an astrobiologist. They just don't know it yet." To look for alien life, she needs all kinds of scientists. She needs scientists to work together. Voytek has spent her life studying life beyond Earth. She'll never quit. She said, "I can't even imagine when it's time to give up. With all the other planets around all the other stars, it's impossible to imagine that life wouldn't have arisen somewhere else."

CHAPTER 5

FIRE AWAY!

There are many reasons why you need fire. First, fire will keep you warm. Second, you can cook with fire. Third, you can use fire to keep aliens away. Fourth, a big fire might be able to blow up the **mothership**. The mothership is the main **UFO**. It's the headquarters. UFO means unidentified flying object.

TIP Make smoke to give you time to run.

HACK

1. Collect a bunch of paper egg cartons.
2. Collect a bunch of dryer **lint**. Lint is fuzz from clothes.
3. Put the dryer lint inside the egg holes.
4. Melt **beeswax**. Beeswax is wax made by honeybees. Pour it over the lint.
5. Tape up the egg cartons.
6. Light it to help start fires.

TIP Make sure that you're safe around fires.

explained by STEM

The key to this hack is beeswax.

Beeswax is a natural wax. It's made by honeybees. Bees collect and use wax. They form cells for storing honey in the hive.

Beeswax is used for many things. It's used as plastic. It's used as a gel. It's used to stop leaks. It's used as polish. It's used for making candles. It can also be eaten.

Beeswax slows the burn time. It burns brighter. It burns longer. It doesn't bend. It burns cleaner. The heat of the flame melts the wax. It turns the melted wax into a hot gas.

DID YOU KNOW?

- The U.S. Air Force studied UFO sightings. The study was from 1947 to 1969. It's known as Project Blue Book. It was the longest U.S. government study of UFOs. It collected over 12,000 UFO sightings. Over 90 percent were "identified." This means they were caused by something known. About 6 percent were "unidentified." This means the cause was unknown. The project had 2 goals. One was to see if UFOs were a threat. Another was to analyze UFO information.

- Stonehenge is a monument of huge stones. Monuments are structures. Stonehenge is located in Wiltshire, England. It's a mystery. Strange things happen around Stonehenge. No one knows how the rocks got there. But some people blame aliens. Aliens are believed to have made Stonehenge. They modeled it after the solar system. They needed a place to land their spaceships.

- Orson Welles was a famous actor. He had a radio show. He told people that Martians were invading New Jersey. He said there were UFOs. He said aliens were firing a heat ray. Many people listened to the show. They believed him. They thought Earth was under attack by aliens. They panicked. Welles felt bad. He said, "It was a terribly shocking experience to realize that I had caused such widespread terror." This happened in 1938.

- SETI stands for Search for Extraterrestrial Intelligence. It's a research organization. It started in 1984. It's in California. Scientists and teachers work there. They study life in the universe. They listen for radio signals. They build tools to search for alien life. They answer the following questions: What is life? How does it begin? Are we alone?

- The Aetherius Society is a religion. It's dedicated to alien intelligence. It was founded by George King. It was founded in 1954. King claimed he was contacted by an alien named Aetherius.

CONSIDER THIS!

TAKE A POSITION!

Which is scarier: an alien invasion or being lost in space? Why? Argue your point with reasons and evidence.

SAY WHAT?

Many of our stories about aliens are based on real science. What is your favorite alien story? Explain how it's based on real science. Create your own science-fiction story.

THINK ABOUT IT!

Many people believe aliens exist. They blame aliens for things we can't explain. For example, strange things happen at the Bermuda Triangle. Some people blame aliens for messing with our tools. They blame aliens for making ships disappear. What would you blame on aliens?

LEARN MORE!

Hoena, Blake, and Paul Fisher-Johnson (illust.). *Can You Survive an Alien Invasion?* North Mankato, MN: Capstone Press, 2016.

Ogden, Charlie. *Surviving an Alien Invasion*. New York, NY: Gareth Stevens Publisher, 2018.

GLOSSARY

airtight (AIR-tite) not letting any air through

aliens (AY-lee-uhns) beings from outer space

battery (BAT-ur-ee) a source of power

beeswax (BEEZ-waks) wax made by honeybees used to build honeycombs in their hives

convection (kuhn-VEK-shuhn) transfer of heat due to the movement of air or water

duct tape (DUHKT TAYP) special tape that is strong, flexible, and waterproof

electrodes (ih-LEK-trodez) conductors through which electricity enters or leaves an object

electrolyte (ih-LEK-truh-lite) a liquid or gel that contains ions and carries electric charges

extraterrestrials (ek-struh-tuh-RES-tree-uhlz) beings from outside Earth

fibers (FYE-burz) tiny threads

filter (FIL-tur) a material that allows things to pass through while keeping unwanted things out

hacks (HAKS) tricks

infect (in-FEKT) to make others sick

insulate (IN-suh-late) to keep warm

lint (LINT) clothes fuzz often found in dryers

mothership (MUHTH-ur SHIP) the main UFO, headquarters

orbit (OR-bit) to move in a curved path around a celestial object

phosphors (FAHS-furz) substances that emit light under a black light

quinine (KWYE-nine) a substance that emits light under a black light

solar (SOH-lur) of the sun

solar systems (SOH-lur SIS-tuhmz) systems that include a sun and all the objects that orbit it

tonic water (TAH-nik WAW-tur) a type of soda with quinine

UFO (YOO-EF-OH) unidentified flying object, a spaceship

UV (YOO-VEE) ultraviolet rays that humans can't see

INDEX